Copyright © 2016 Virginia Gail Reed.

All rights reserved. No part of this book may be used or reproduced by any means, graphic, electronic, or mechanical, including photocopying, recording, taping or by any information storage retrieval system without the written permission of the author except in the case of brief quotations embodied in critical articles and reviews.

Archway Publishing books may be ordered through booksellers or by contacting:

Archway Publishing
1663 Liberty Drive
Bloomington, IN 47403
www.archwaypublishing.com
1 (888) 242-5904

Because of the dynamic nature of the Internet, any web addresses or links contained in this book may have changed since publication and may no longer be valid. The views expressed in this work are solely those of the author and do not necessarily reflect the views of the publisher, and the publisher hereby disclaims any responsibility for them.

Any people depicted in stock imagery provided by Thinkstock are models, and such images are being used for illustrative purposes only.
Certain stock imagery © Thinkstock.

ISBN: 978-1-4808-3587-0 (sc)
ISBN: 978-1-4808-3632-7 (hc)
ISBN: 978-1-4808-3588-7 (e)

Printed in the United States.

Archway Publishing rev. date: 11/17/2016

This Book Belongs To

_____

An Extraordinary Lady

Of

Impeccable Character!

A Gift From

_____

Contents

Girls Are "Special" 1
Good Morning Sunshine! 2
Introductions and Greetings 3
Powder Room Responsibilities 4
Attitude and Spreading Rumors 5
Are You A Good Sport? 6
Values and Being Considerate 7
Eye Contact and Polite Conversation 8
The Magic Words 9
Be A Classy Lady! 10
Accepting Responsibility 11
Respect! 12
Self-Control and Communication Skills 13
Table Manners 14
Bullying and Cyberbullying 15
Decisions . . . Decisions! 16
Good Character Is Important! 17

Dedication

This book is dedicated to all mothers and fathers who strive to instill courteous and respectful values in their children and to the readers of this book who honor their parents by using courteous behaviors.

To my mother and father, Virginia and Bill Hilliard, who gave me such a wonderful childhood and taught me what was really important in life.

To the ladies in my life . . . my grandmother, Eula Stone, mother-in-law, Elizabeth Reed, daughters, Shelli Hopkins and Whitney Gaines, granddaughters, Adley and Claire Gaines, sisters, Susan Harmon and June McTaggart, sister-in-law, Alicia Lanae, nieces, Amber Rundquist, Jennifer Harmon, April Beckman, and Elizabeth Arthur.

Practicing the art of good manners starts in the home. Teaching children good manners must begin at an early age and these behaviors reinforced until they become second nature. Instilling good manners in a child is one of the most important responsibilities a parent will ever have. This book is meant to grow with your child because teaching manners is an ongoing process. It is also meant to encourage dialogue with you and your daughter in learning proper social behavior.

Girls Are "Special" . . .

    Young ladies should have courteous and respectful behavior because having nice manners is very important and gives distinction to every female. Knowing the proper way to conduct yourself in social situations shows that you have good etiquette . . . or proper manners.

Good Morning Sunshine!

Girls enjoy feeling as fresh as a daisy! Your morning routine should include brushing your teeth, washing your face, combing and styling your hair, and showering if needed. Everyone wants to have fresh breath and smell nice and clean, so be aware of this. Dress yourself in clean clothes and do your best to look neat and presentable.

When you get up in the morning and see your mother, father, sister, or brother, always remember to say "Good morning!" This can be difficult if you are not a morning person, but acknowledging others is the right thing to do. A simple "Good morning" sets the tone for a positive day! Be sure that you give your teachers and friends a friendly smile and warm greeting regardless of whether or not you are having a good day. This good habit and positive attitude will make your day go better!

Introductions and Greetings

First impressions are important . . . you only have one chance to make a good first impression! If you are meeting a person for the first time be sure to extend your hand and give them a firm handshake. Be pleasant, speak with a positive tone in your voice, use direct eye contact, and call the person by name when you tell them, "It is nice to meet you!" If you do not know their name . . . ask! Say, "Hello, my name is (your name), and what is your name?" When shaking hands, please do not let your hand feel like a limp noodle . . . grip their hand firmly and confidently. Following these simple guidelines will help you make a good first impression.

It is also important for you to respond when another person enters a room or comes into your presence. You should stop what you are doing and acknowledge that person immediately.

Powder Room Responsibilities

Respect the rights of others to privacy and cleanliness. Always knock before entering if the bathroom door is closed. If you have an accident and make a mess it is your responsibility to clean it up before you leave! Do not hog the toilet or bathroom, especially if there is only one in the house. If soap, toilet paper, or a clean towel is needed, be sure that you replace it. Girls, be sure to wear a bathrobe or a towel to and from the shower as modest behavior may keep you from an embarrassing situation. Always flush the toilet, dispose of your feminine products in the proper manner, and wash and dry your hands thoroughly. If you take a bath or shower do not forget to hang up your towel, put your clothes in the dirty clothes hamper, and leave the area neat and clean. Be sure not to take too long in the bathroom . . . be considerate of others that are waiting.

Attitude and Spreading Rumors

Show enthusiasm . . . it is very contagious! People do not enjoy being around a dull and uninteresting person all the time. Show your passion for the things that you love. Be aware of your attitude . . . your attitude can be negative, unfriendly, and pessimistic . . . or you can have an attitude of being positive, friendly, and optimistic. Be sympathetic, considerate, and constructive in the things you say and do. Disrespectful actions such as rolling your eyes, refusing to look at someone's face, and walking away while someone is talking to you are discourteous and demonstrate a poor attitude. Being cocky is not cool! Nobody likes a smart aleck or a know-it-all. Mind your own business and take no part in drama! Many times girls can be mean and you do not want to have any part of being cruel or ugly to anybody! The way that you treat other people and how you make them feel about themselves speaks volumes about the kind of person you are. Be kind . . . do not pry or ask personal questions, boast about yourself, talk about money issues, or compare and criticize people. Be considerate of others while being true to yourself.

Do not spread rumors or tattle on other people. This kind of action is hurtful and unkind and you would never intentionally torment another person. Think carefully before you speak words that may cause hurt feelings. Remember the Golden Rule . . . "Do unto others as you would have them do unto you."

Are You A Good Sport?

Show good sportsmanship at all times and never be more aggressive than necessary. If someone falls down, help him or her up. No one likes a sore loser! Tell your opponents, "Good game," and do not brag if you are on the winning team. It is fine to be happy that you won, but do not celebrate winning in a way that hurts anyone's feelings. Also, NEVER boo the opposing team . . . this shows poor sportsmanship as well as poor character! Always thank the coach and referees and shake hands with your opponents at the end of the game. If the national anthem plays, stand up, take off your hat, and turn towards the flag to show respect. If you lose a game, accept the defeat gracefully . . . even when playing board games! Be truthful and do not cheat. Showing that you have integrity is a major part of being a good sport.

When playing team sports show others that you are a team player by the way you conduct yourself during a game. Share the ball . . . do not be a ball hog!! Cheer for your teammates and be supportive. You play on a team . . . it is not a one-man show! If someone steals the ball, as in basketball or soccer, do not be angry with your opponent . . . just play harder. Show good sportsmanship by playing aggressively within the rules of the game.

Values and Being Considerate

Girls, stand your ground and know how you feel about topics such as integrity (honesty), trust, loyalty, ambition, tolerance, and self-respect. Learn to speak up for yourself and others in the face of injustice and believe in your innate goodness. Have confidence and listen to the wisdom of your inner voice. Know what you believe and stand by your beliefs. Do not let other people change your values or make you feel that your views are wrong. Have an open mind and listen to others, but be true to yourself and your values. Always hold your head high . . . but never your nose. Be humble and have an attitude of gratitude. Empower other people through gentleness, compassion, and consideration of the needs of others. True beauty begins on the inside.

Hold the door open and allow older people or children to go inside first. A good rule to remember is . . . "Ladies and babies go first!" When preceding others into a building, do not let the door slam in the face of those behind you. Instead, hold the door until it can be reached. This reflects courteous and respectful behavior! When another person opens or holds the door for you, remember to acknowledge this kindness and say, "Thank you."

Eye Contact and Polite Conversation

It is so important to look people directly in the eyes if you are talking to them or if they are talking to you. This visual contact with another person shows respect and that you are truly interested in what that person has to say. It also lets them know that you are sincere in what you are saying to them. In this age of smartphones and constant digital connection, your undivided attention is one of the highest compliments you can give another person.

If there are several people involved in a conversation, please make sure that everyone feels included . . . no one wants to be left out of a discussion. Learn to include instead of exclude others. An "includer," is a person who is good at bringing people in and making them feel a part of things. When conversing do not monopolize or do all of the talking . . . let others share their ideas.

Do not interrupt a person when he or she is talking. Wait for them to finish what they are saying and then speak. If someone makes a mistake, kindly point it out to him or her privately. Do not embarrass any person in front of others.

Keep the drama under control, and be aware of your tone. The manner in which you speak to others should be polite and positive, which will be much better received than being harsh or angry. Remember that conversation is a life skill and art that needs daily practice.

The Magic Words

Remember to say, "Yes, ma'am" and "No, ma'am" or "Yes, sir" and "No, sir" (or just "Yes, please" and "No, thank you" if customary). These words simply show that you are being polite and respectful. Do not forget to say, "Please, thank you, you're welcome, and excuse me," as these are courteous words that all classy ladies use.

Writing a thank-you note is another way of showing respect for someone who has done something kind for you. This lets that person know how much you appreciate their thoughtfulness. If you do not respond to a kind act, then you are being insensitive and inconsiderate. Give the person a phone call, send an email, or a personal visit thanking them as this action is very much appreciated as well as expected. Showing gratitude by writing the individual and expressing your feelings exhibits genuine kindness and sincerity. If you receive a gift and you already have the exact same item, remember to be gracious and thank the person who gave you the present . . . never remark that you already have one.

Be sure to remember to RSVP to an invitation. This means that you should let the host or hostess know if you plan to attend. The individual was kind enough to include you as a guest, so you certainly should be considerate enough to let them know if you intend to be present or if you are unable to attend.

Be A Classy Lady!

Girls . . . all people appreciate kindness so be sure to open the door for people older than you, use proper language in their presence, offer them your chair if no other seats are available, and be helpful by offering assistance if needed. This is especially thoughtful if the person is in a wheelchair, on crutches, or pushing a baby stroller. Show that you are considerate, tolerant, and respectful of others. Sit up straight, keep your knees together, or sit tall with your legs gently crossed at the knee or ankle. This good posture will help you feel feminine, graceful, and classy.

Try really hard NOT to embarrass anyone. What may seem humorous and teasing could be very embarrassing to another person. Always think how you would feel under those circumstances. If you ever wonder about the right thing to do . . . ALWAYS choose kindness. Be intelligent and considerate, but not a know-it-all!

Remember to dress with respect. Just because a certain fashion is in style does not mean it is appropriate for you. Consult a responsible adult if you are unsure. Use good judgment and always wear age-appropriate clothing and make-up. Always remember, a smile is the prettiest thing you could ever wear . . . and all people smile in the same language.

Accepting Responsibility

Always take responsibility for the things you say and do. If you do something wrong admit your mistake, say you are sorry, and make every effort to prevent it from happening again. We all make mistakes, but you must acknowledge your errors and accept responsibility for your actions. If consequences are imposed, take them with a good and positive attitude and learn from the experience.

Keep your room tidy and be quick to volunteer to help around the house and in the kitchen. You should make your bed, pick up your belongings, and keep your room organized. Keep your parents informed about your schoolwork so they can assist you when you need help. It is your job to complete your homework assignments and turn them in on or before the due date. You will gain the admired distinction of being a reliable young lady by being prompt and fulfilling expectations. Do NOT keep people waiting on you . . . strive to be punctual for every activity!

Respect!

Respect the space of other family members by being considerate, tolerant, and understanding. Never ramble through someone's private possessions without permission and be discreet by keeping family affairs private. Be as good as your word . . . when you say that you are going to do something . . . then do it with no excuses!

Be particularly aware of treating your elders with honor and respect. Offer them your seat and allow them to go first in line. Older people have much wisdom and you can learn many valuable lessons by taking the time to listen to what they have to say.

Remember to thank the men and women that serve in the military. Express gratitude for their service and acknowledge their contributions that keep our country free. Be aware that you may be the one wearing that uniform one day.

Be grateful for the law enforcement officers and first responders that protect you and your community. These brave individuals who strive to keep us safe deserve our gratitude and respect.

Self-Control and Communication Skills

Do not lose your temper easily or use language that is inappropriate as this shows poor self-control. Instead, learn to manage your emotions in a positive way. The use of offensive language is never appropriate as it only reveals poor character and a limited vocabulary. DO NOT tattle on others (unless they are in danger), spread rumors that hurt people, or make fun of people who are different. Be aware of what your body language is saying . . . rolling your eyes, clinching your fist, stamping your feet, having a scowl on your face, or pouting shows poor self-control. When shopping with your parents make sure to stay close, do not plead for toys, or run and play in the store. Show that you are well behaved by controlling what you say and do.

Effective face-to-face communication skills are essential to success in life. The ability to convey your thoughts and feelings is important. Be aware that words such as "like" and "you know" are often overused. Be certain that the words you use are chosen carefully and intelligently . . . think before you speak. You should NOT play video games, text, or talk on the phone in inappropriate places. The number of "likes" you may get on Instagram or Facebook does not measure true success! Use good communication skills to enhance your life with your friends and those you work with daily.

Table Manners

Having good table manners should be a way of life. Before having a meal, it would be considerate to offer to help set the table. When you are seated be sure to place your napkin in your lap and you should not start eating until everyone else has been served. Use nice table manners . . . DO NOT place your elbows on the table, chew with your mouth open, speak with food in your mouth, or discuss inappropriate topics. Pass food as requested from left to right and never say that you don't like a particular dish. Just say, "I do not care for any thank you." When everyone is finished, place your napkin beside your plate, your utensils across your plate, and always tell your host or hostess that you enjoyed the meal and ask if you may be excused. It would be thoughtful to offer to help clear the table. NEVER call attention to another person's poor manners.

When dining out, do not disturb other people who are there to enjoy their meal. Remain in your seat, speak in a quiet tone, STAY OFF of your cell phone or electronic devices, and show courtesy toward the person serving you. Polite manners are expected from a *lady* . . . and that is exactly what you are!

Bullying and Cyberbullying

Girls, stand up for a person that is being put down or bullied. DO NOT allow bullying to take place at any time when you are with your friends or acquaintances. Support your friends and inspire them. However, please be aware that you must always be certain that your friend's words and actions are worthy of your encouragement and support. When in doubt, always choose to be kind. This includes your communications on social media.

Cyberbullying that involves inappropriate texts, pictures, or email is NEVER acceptable. If you receive a threatening electronic communication from anyone, seek assistance from an adult as soon as possible. DO NOT share your personal information, send a photo of yourself, make hurtful or threatening remarks, or plan to see a stranger you met online. For your own safety, make your parents aware of all of your online activities! Learn to communicate effectively inside and outside the world of technology. Electronic communication is wonderful but there is no substitute for face-to-face conversation. Always stand up for what is right when it involves your safety in online activities.

Decisions . . . Decisions!

You make many choices every day. You decide what clothes you wear, what food you will eat, whether or not you will do your homework, or how you spend your free time. The choices you make define your character and become your life. You know right from wrong and you know good from bad . . . but if you need help, do not be afraid to ask an adult for guidance.

Be a good role model as well as a good friend. Others are watching and learning from your actions. Choose your friends very carefully and select those with like values. Friends should bring out the best in you. You do not have to be close friends with everyone, but you have a responsibility to be respectful to everybody. Make your own choices . . . do not follow others blindly.

Make the decision to have a compassionate heart for others. All people face different challenges and difficulties. Do not always think or talk about yourself. Let other people know that you care about what they are dealing with in life. No matter how educated, talented, or wealthy you are, the way you treat people reflects the kind of person you really are.

Good Character Is Important!

Character is defined as the way someone thinks, feels, and behaves. Simply put, it is the way you act when no one is looking. Having good character indicates moral strength and is a positive personality trait. The friends you make, how successful you are in the career path you select, and even the attraction of your ideal spouse later in life will be determined by your character and good manners. The polite way that you treat others and the courteous actions you choose will put you on an appropriate and positive path in life. Your character is reflected in the way you treat other people . . . always treat others with kindness, respect, and civility. Our world would be so much better if everyone practiced this! Remember that perseverance, which is the quality that allows someone to try to do something even though it is difficult, and hard work will pay off. Strive to be the best that you can be and take great pride in all that you do.

H onor your Mother and Father, or that special person who takes care of you, by being kind and considerate to others. Good manners are perceived immediately. Young ladies should be pretty on the "inside" by the way they speak and act . . . this is essential for every girl to know. Always be kind to others, because everyone is facing a battle that you may know nothing about. Showing kindness to others is your special gift to them!

Using courteous and polite skills, otherwise known as proper etiquette or good manners, will easily identify you as a . . .

"Very Special and Extraordinary Young Lady!"

G irls, learn to listen intelligently with your heart and use
good judgment . . . you are a gift to this world!

In The List Below, Which Manners Do You Know And Use Every Day?

I speak to people in the morning.
I brush my teeth and keep my body clean.
I look people in the eyes when I talk to them.
I give a firm handshake when I meet someone.

I knock before entering a room when the door is closed.
I leave the bathroom neat and clean.
I do not roll my eyes when I disagree with a person.
I do not act like a smart aleck or a know-it-all.

I keep my mouth closed if I do not have a kind word to say.
I do not walk away from a person that is talking to me.
I am a good sport and congratulate the team that wins.
I do not boo the opposing team or have unkind things to say.

I do not brag if my team wins.
I do not hog the ball and try to be a team player at all times.
I accept losing in good grace.
I remember the rule, "Ladies and babies go first!"

I never ramble through another person's possessions.
I do not tattle on my friends unless there is danger involved.
I offer my elders a chair if they do not have one.
I try to include all people that are involved in a discussion.

I say, "Yes, ma'am, no, ma'am, yes, sir, and no, sir, or yes/no."
I write thank-you notes when I receive a gift.
I say, "Please, thank you, you're welcome, and excuse me."
I use proper language in the presence of adults and friends.

I take responsibility for the things I say and do.
I make up my bed and keep my room tidy.
I dress with respect.
I help out with chores around the house.
I turn in assignments on time and take pride in a job well done.

I inform my parents of upcoming deadlines.
I respect my family, adults, seniors, and those in uniform.
I control my body language and use self-control at all times.
I never make fun of people who are different.

I do not plead for toys or run and play in stores.
I use my electronic devices and cell phone in appropriate places.
I strive to be punctual and on time for all commitments.
I do not use electronic devices during a meal.

I do not overuse words such as "like" or "you know."
I wait until everyone is served before eating.
I do not allow bullying to take place in my presence.
I tell my parents if I receive improper texts, email, or tweets.

I remember to RSVP to all invitations.
I do not boast or talk only about myself.
I sit up straight, tall, and ladylike.
I NEVER give out my personal information online.

I try to make good choices knowing that it will affect my future.
I hold my head high, but never my nose.
I stop what I am doing and acknowledge a person that enters.
I honor my Mother and Father by being kind and considerate.

I have a compassionate heart.
I strive to be considerate, tolerant, and respectful.
I keep family affairs private.
I strive to hold true to my values of trust, integrity and loyalty.

I can and will be . . .

A Very "Special and Extraordinary" Young Lady!

Third in a series of five books on manners
for children, teens, and adults.

I Can't Find My Manners
Manners and More for Boys
Manners and More for Girls
Manners and More for Little Ones
Manners at the Theater for Young People

For information about the books or
to order books please visit my website

mannersbooks.com

**Gail Reed
Author**

Gail Reed, a retired educator of forty-two years, lives in Evans, Georgia, with her husband, Travis. She earned her Bachelor of Science degree in Education from the University of Georgia, Master of Education degree from Augusta University, and Specialist in Education degree from the University of Georgia. Gail feels blessed with a wonderful family. She has two adult daughters, Shelli and Whitney, and two sweet granddaughters, Adley and Claire. While growing up, Gail loved wearing pretty dresses that would twirl when she would spin around and loved to play dress up. She loved lace and frills yet enjoyed wearing her cowboy boots when riding her horse. Today young ladies should be taught that having nice manners and developing good character is very important. The life lessons discussed in *Manners and More for Girls* will help little girls develop into delightful young ladies that make their parents very proud.

**Carrie Brooks
Illustrator**

Carrie Brooks comes from a family of artists. She knew from a young age she wanted to be an artist when she grew up. Her earliest memories are of watching her mother make dolls in her art studio and her dad work in his woodshop at home. Most of her childhood centered on being creative, building forts in the woods, fostering stray animals, and playing dress up with her two sisters, Katie and Stephanie, and her friend and neighbor, Victory. In 2002, she graduated from the University of Georgia with a Bachelor of Fine Arts in Art and Art Education; Carrie has taught art, photography, and ceramics for fifteen years, the last seven years at Lakeside High School (her alma mater). While in college, Carrie studied art in Cortona, Italy, which inspired her love of travel. Each summer she travels to a new destination with her students which often influences her artwork in unexpected ways. In 2008, she earned her Master of Education degree from Lesley University. Many of the illustrations in this book were inspired by the likenesses of her friends' children and her nieces, Mary and Sophia. Carrie lives in Martinez, Georgia, with her husband, Bo, and their seven cats, some of which are included in this book.

Illustrator photograph by Mary Scheirer